Content

Dedication:

Thank you, to my Lord and Savior; for giving me the desire and skill-set to have a vision to help guide others.

Thank you to my Wife, (Crystal Danyel); for the love, patience, and support while I spent the time and effort developing the contents of this project.

Thank you to my mentors and supporters; for every opportunity you imparted wisdom into me, preparing me to be the same for others.

Thank you, Lincoln & Hill, for the continued autonomy to convert your training & skill development projects from idea to fruition for replication.

Tags & Legend

Action Time Tag: depicts individuals or a couple must

physically move on principle learned

Active Listening Tag: depicts one individual should be actively

listening each time another individual is talking in the communication

process

Advice Tag: depicts information from confidant for

emphasizing key point

Agitator Tag: depicts a person or organization that incites the

emotions of others through positive or negative information

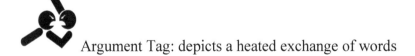 Argument Tag: depicts a heated exchange of words

Audio Commentary tag: depicts a piece of supplementary audio

information

Back against the wall Tag: depicts unfavorable circumstances;

past, present, and foreseeable future

Behavior-Illicit Tag: depicts illegal behavior that is tolerance

driven

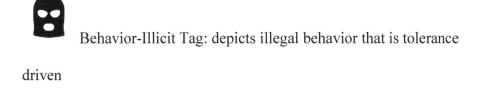 Behavior-Inherited Tag: depicts behavior that is instinctively

driven

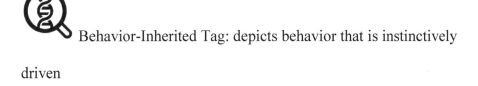 Behavior-Surrounding Tag: depicts behavior that is

environmentally driven

Behavior-Taught Tag: depicts behavior that is learned

progressively

Beyond Superficial Tag: depicts behavior or actions below what is visible seen

Beyond the Box Tag: depicts behaviors, thoughts, actions outside normal scope of individuals or group

Big Brother Tag: depicts an organization or government could be observing you

Bird's Eye Tag: depicts a deeper look into a subject surrounding a person, place or thing

Booking Tag: depicts an opportunity to for a speaker is available

Booty Call Tag: depicts a sexual encounter that's counterproductive to relationships

Caution Tag: depicts the subject or information should be approached carefully

Caught-up Tag: depicts an action that directly resulted in negative circumstances

Caveat Tag: depicts a specific threat when considering additional information about this subject

Challenge Tag: depicts individuals or a couple must complete an assignment immediately before moving to next concept

Championed Tag: depicts a social philosophy that is influencing others positively or negatively

Change Tag: depicts a personal evolution that is forced or natural

Checkpoint Tag: depicts a location gauge during subject or individual progression

Coach Tag: depicts a personal philosophy is available to be learned

Commentary Tag: depicts supplementary data through public research & discussions that we may oppose or support subject but used for teaching purposes

Communicate Tag: depicts general subject matter verbalized between male & female cohorts

Concert Rose Tag: depicts positivity birth in-spite of the harshest circumstances or surroundings

Connection Tag: depicts a link to other materials available through the Lincoln & Hill Training suite

Content tag: depicts supplementary data through public research & discussions that we may oppose or support but use for teaching

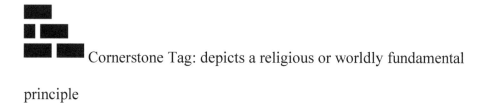 Cornerstone Tag: depicts a religious or worldly fundamental

principle

Critisism Tag: depicts openly negative chastising for founded or

unfounded reasons

Dictionary Tag: depicts words or phrases that are not considered

common

Directional Tag: depicts perceived versus true direction of moral

compass

Discipleship Tag: depicts lesson that require a mentor/mentee

relationship

Discussion Tag: depicts specific subject matter verbalized

between male & female cohorts

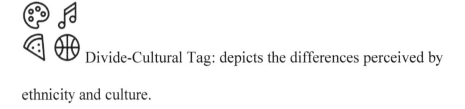 Divide-Cultural Tag: depicts the differences perceived by

ethnicity and culture.

Divide-Digital Tag: depicts the differences perceived by access

to or /lack of global information

Divide-Economical Tag: depicts the differences perceived by

financial assets and net-worth

Divide-Educational Tag: depicts the differences perceived by

access to and completion of higher education

Divide-Legal Tag: depicts the differences perceived by

interaction with the legal system

Divide-Racial Tag: depicts the differences perceived by outer physical appearance

Divide-Political Tag: depicts the differences perceived by political affiliation

Divide-Spiritual Tag: depicts the differences seen based on religious practices

Dysfunctional Tag: depicts the taught process, actions or behaviors that conflict with appropriate (by general standards) responses.

End-of-Rope Tag: depicts the end of human strength and the beginning of God's strength

Entertainment-Public Tag: depicts social enactments outside the dwelling

Entertainment-Private Tag: depicts social enactments inside the dwelling

Equity Tag: depicts the resources & opportunity to succeed is evenly distributed based on need

Evangelism Tag: depicts the opportunity to spread the good news

Examine Heart Tag: depicts a circumstance that will harden or soften the heart

Ex Tag: depicts a person, a place or thing from your past

Fast Forward Tag: depicts visualization of the future direction of individuals dictated by actions taken

Film Tag: depicts supplementary data through developed negative footage to support or refute a philosophy or teaching

Flow Control Tag: depicts the people or organizations that desire to control the ebb & flow of information or policies that influence other people

Forces-Seen Tag: depicts tangible human opposition

Forces-Unseen Tag: depicts intangible spiritual opposition

Gender-Female Tag: depicts the actions of a female has transpired

Gender-Male Tag: depicts the actions of a male has transpired

Gender-Man Tag: depicts the actions of a man is required

Gender-Woman Tag: depicts the actions of a woman is required

Go back Tag: depicts individuals or a couple is required to review a subject already mentioned

Healing Tag: depicts a person, a place or thing that can help start the healing process.

Hearing the Word Tag: depicts the individually or corporately heard proclamations of the scriptures

Hermeneutics Nugget Tag: depicts individuals or a couple should further research & study the theological interpretation in a scripturally accurate context

High Priority Tag: depicts critical information or concept in specific session or chapters about a subject

Hope Tag: depicts a person, a place or thing that provides reassurance or confidence to the hopeless

Household Tag: depicts a situation that should be handled within the home

Hustle with a Strategy Tag: depicts making calculated moves beyond the bare minimum required

Impression Tag: depicts the imprint left behind by your words or actions

In-the-Ditch Tag: depicts a previous choice that has put a person or people in an immoral situation or at a disadvantage

Influenced Tag: depicts the people, places or things that individuals get swayed by

Influencer Tag: depicts the people, places or things that sway other individuals

Inner Struggle Tag: depicts opposing options are available but only one can be selected

Insignia Tag: depicts individuals or related to the legacy associated with a family or generation

Investigate Tag: depicts individuals or a couple should further research & study subject matter

Issue-Educational Tag: depicts an issue pertaining to the education system

Issue-Financial Tag: depicts an issue pertaining to the economic system

Issue-Judicial Tag: depicts an issue pertaining the justice system

Issue-Political Tag: depicts an issue pertaining to the political process

Issue-Social Tag: depicts an issue pertaining to social injustices

Issue-Systematic Tag: depicts an issue pertaining to the

systematic impediment of individuals or groups

Key Point Tag: depicts main topics covered in specific subject,

session or chapter

Life Hack Tag: depicts a strategy or technique adopted to

manage time and activities more efficiently

The LIFE project Tag: depicts principles associated with

Lincoln & Hill Training's reentry curricula

Lighthouse Tag: depicts being a valid example within God's

will

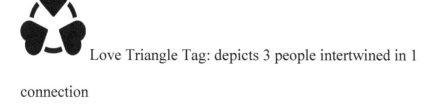 Love Triangle Tag: depicts 3 people intertwined in 1

connection

Man-Code Tag: depicts unwritten or unspoken thinking, manners or actions held true by male gender even without evidence of validity

Memory Tag: depicts a verse or passage recommended for memorization

Measured Tag: depicts the qualitative or quantitative results of circumstances portrayed or observed

Microscope Tag: depicts extreme observation will take place as a result of past or present actions

Motivational Tag: depicts more energy is needed to prevail in current circumstances

Move Away Tag: depicts a person, place or thing you should depart from immediately

Nugget Tag: depicts more information can be learned about a person, a place or thing with a desire to dig deeper

Opportunity Tag: depicts an opening to gain, grow or monetize a situation previously unseen to you

Parental Tag: depicts a decision must be made with the best interest of the child/children at its core

Pass the Baton Tag: depicts ideas and concepts related to changing of the guard in a legacy

Pause Tag: depicts taking a break within a situation to rethink direction before proceeding

Personal SWOT Analysis Tag: depicts taking an inventory of your situation before making a life altering decision

Pivot Point Tag: depicts a juncture that the movement required, changes the trajectory permanently

Plan Tag: depicts individuals or a couple have written procedures to follow

Play Tag: depicts the attempt to try a circumstance for the first time to accomplish a new skill or information

Playing the Fool Tag: depicts willingly or unwillingly tolerating the foolishness of others

Policy Tag: depicts written documents that negatively affect the lives of specific individuals and communities

Positive/Negative Tag: depicts the current situation has a 50/50 potential of going either direction

Power Imbalance Tag: depicts the potentially imbalance of power or influence in a relationship (personal or professional)

Power of Tounge Tag: depicts the positive or negative impact an individual's words carry

Practical Exercise Tag: depicts individuals or a couple must complete an assignment before next session can proceed

Prayer Tag: depicts the need for the power of prayer is imminent

Prerequisite Tag: depicts requirements prior to starting something

Problem Solver Tag: depicts critical thinking skills used to complete an previously unsolved task or circumstance

Promiscuous Tag: depicts indiscriminate behaviors, thoughts, actions outside the normal scope of relationships

Quick Start Tag: depicts an individual or couple addressing a subject or request with first thought (no extra time for contemplating better answer)

Rat Race Tag: depicts the traps of corporate America that requires some form of sacrifice

Read It Tag: depicts a lesson or information that requires reading or learning

Recharge Tag: depicts a need to refresh your body, mind or spirit

Red Handed Tag: depicts being caught in the act

Reflection Tag: depicts individuals thinking about subject or questions before providing an answer

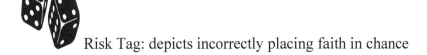 Replay Tag: depicts the attempt to retry a circumstance from the past to accomplish a different outcome without new skills or information

Resource Tag: depicts a form of information available to supplement a concept

Rewind Tag: depicts the attempt to review the past to reflect on mistakes

Risk Tag: depicts incorrectly placing faith in chance

Sand of Time Tag: depicts individuals or a couple must make a time sensitive decision to proceed

Scripture Tag: depicts a cross-reference to another biblical passage in correct context of meaning

Self-Discipline Tag: depicts a control of self during

circumstances outside of the individual's controllability

 Skip Tag: depicts the attempt to bypass steps in the process

 Sphere-Friendship Tag: depicts the sphere of influence

dictated by the associates selected

 Sphere-Home Tag: depicts the sphere of influence dictated by

parental training

 Sphere-World Tag: depicts the sphere of influence dictated by

the world

 Snooze-U-Lose Tag: depicts slow acting or thinking resulting in

opportunities being missed

Steps Ordered Tag: depicts divine intervention in the direction currently being followed

Temptation Tag: depicts a person, a place or things that is a potential hindrance to an objective

Testimony Tag: depicts a former test that requires sharing of a testament of survival

Transferred Knowledge Tag: depicts information shared with the next generation

Under the Radar Tag: depicts a subject that is going unnoticed purposely or unintentionally

Video Tag: depicts supplementary data through digital footage to support or refute a philosophy or teaching

Visionary Tag: depicts seeing beyond what is currently present to support something bigger

 Watchman Tag: depicts a person/mentee could be observing how you behave or respond

Woo Tag: depicts attempting to physically or mentally influence an individual temporarily

Works Tag: depicts individual toil is the reasoning for successes, influence or impact

Digital Security Protocols

The call for and desire of heightened security and privacy measures has led to several protocols and standards being developed. Among these are:

1. Secure Socket Layer (SSL) which is a standard security protocol for establishing encrypted links between a web server and a browser in an online communication. SSL technology ensures all data transmitted remains encrypted.

2. Transport Layer Security (TLS) which is a protocol that provides communication security between client/server applications that communicate with each other over the Internet. Enabling privacy, integrity and protection for the data that's transmitted between different nodes.

3. Secure IP (IPSec) which is a set of protocols that provides security for Internet Protocol. IPsec can be used for the setting up of virtual private networks (VPNs) in a secure manner.

4. Secure HTTP (S-HTTP) which is an extension to the Hypertext Transfer Protocol (HTTP) that allows the secure exchange of files on the World Wide Web.

5. Secure E-mail (PGP and S/MIME)

   a. Pretty Good Privacy (PGP) which is an encryption program that provides cryptographic privacy and authentication for data communication. PGP is used for signing, encrypting, and decrypting texts, e-mails, files, directories, and whole disk partitions and to increase the security of e-mail communications.

   b. S/MIME (Secure Multi-Purpose Internet Mail Extensions) which is a secure method of sending e-mail that uses an encryption system. S/MIME is included in the latest versions of the Web browsers from Microsoft and Netscape and has also been endorsed by other vendors that make messaging products.

6. DNDSEC, the Domain Name System Security Extensions is a suite of Internet Engineering Task Force (IETF) specifications for securing certain kinds of information provided by the Domain Name System (DNS).

7. SSH, the protocol (also referred to as the Secure Shell) is a method for secure remote login from one computer to another. It provides several alternative options for strong authentication, and it protects the communications security and integrity with strong encryption.

OSI Model

The Open Systems Interconnection (OSI) Model is an abstract layout that describes network communication used on open systems for connectivity. The OSI model encompasses seven subcomponents, effectively called layers. Each layer represents a group of services provided to the adjoining layers. The OSI model helps deliver the protocols for the security and privacy measures.

Seven Layers

The International Standards Organization (ISO) developed the OSI model. The model is divided into seven network communication layers. Layers 1 through 4 are considered the lower layers, concerned with the movement of data. Layers 5 through 7, the upper layers, contain application-level data.

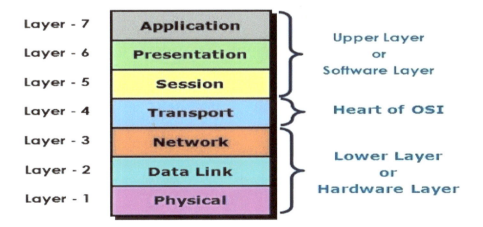

- Layer 7 (application)

  The application Layer is at the top; as the user, interfaces with it. Applications that work at Layer 7 engage the users responsively. The general terms the user presses a button and the layer interacts with the computer functions directly.

- Layer 6 (presentation)

  The Presentation Layer represents the area that is independent of data representation at the application layer. This layer represents the preparation or translation of application format to network format, or from network formatting to application formatting.

- Layer 5 (session)

  When two devices, computers or servers need to "speak" with each another, a session needs to be created. The sessions are done at the Session Layer. Functionality at this layer involves setup, coordination, and termination between the applications at each end of the session.

- Layer 4 (transport)

  The Transport Layer handles the coordination of the data transfer between end-systems and hosts. The coordination of how much data to send, at what rate, and where it goes. The best-known Transport Layer is the Transmission Control Protocol (TCP), which is built on top of the Internet Protocol (IP), commonly

known as TCP/IP.

- Layer 3 (network)

  The Network Layer in its most basic sense, is responsible for

  packet forwarding, including routing through different routers.

- Layer 2 (data link)

  The Data Link Layer provides node-to-node data transfer (between

  two directly connected nodes) also handling error correction from

  the physical layer. Two sublayers exist on this level, the Media

  Access Control (MAC) layer and the Logical Link Control (LLC)

  layer respectfully.

- Layer 1 (physical)

  At the bottom of the OSI is the Physical Layer, which represents the electrical and physical representation of the system. This can include everything from the cable type, radio frequency link, as well as the layout of pins, voltages and other physical requirements.

The OSI security architecture model operates in a parallel design with seven layers. These layers reflect the highest view of the different requirements within network security.

OSI Model	Security Model
Application	Authentication
Presentation	Access Control
Session	Non-Repudiation
Transport	Data Integrity
Network	Confidentiality
Data Link	Assurance / Availability
Physical	Notarization / Signature

At this juncture, security limits unauthorized personnel the access to information but a digital footprint of activities continues to build for every encounter through the world-wide web. The common link between systems failure and intentional attacks is the human factor.

Human Factor

When it comes to security, the human factor often scores higher than any threat posed by technology. The hardest element to control in having an impenetrable system is the end-users, because their behaviors are not predictable but often detectable. Misbehaving employees account for a prominent number of security fears.

Passwords

It is believed in the Cyber Security world that, "the weakest link in cyber security is the human being." The perception also makes the human factor the lowest hanging fruit, translating to many of the opportunities to inflict problems are targeting uninformed people. Passwords are the first line of defense in protecting the digital footprint but often the one human factor is the least protected. Many users believe their passwords should be simple and share them across professional, personal, and social media accounts. This approach is dangerous because if one falls, the rest of them come down eventually. The symptom is training yourself to create strong, memorable, unique passwords. The process can be accomplished by follow these steps:

Step 1: Create an easy to remember but strong password core.

- Choose a memorable phrase to you, e.g. Mary had a little lamb

- Take the initials from that phrase: Mhall

- Now choose a second one, e.g. The early bird gets the worm

- Take the initials from this second phrase: Tebgtw

- Combine them with a memorable special character, like an ampersand (&) or a plus sign (+)

- Result: Mhall+Tebgtw

Step 2: Create an easy to remember variable password Core

- You have many choices here. The easiest is to create variant of the account to which you are logging in.

- Make the variable component (3 letters of source)

Step 3: Combine the Core and variable creating memorable/strong password.

- Core + Variable = strong and easy to remember

- You can again combine them using another special character.

Cookies

The Cookie is a packet of data sent by an Internet server to a browser. The packet is returned by the browser each time it accesses the same server, used to identify the user or track their access to the server. When browsers lack integrity through their cookie verification, it opens the possibility of hackers extracting supposedly encrypted information from those connections.

Cyber Attacks

A cyber-attack is a deliberate attempt by a hacker to impair or stop a computer network or system from functioning. The list of cyber-attacks and threats is becoming extensive, but these are the most common typically in some form or combination, research yourself for more specific information:

- Advanced Persistent Threats (APT) is a prolonged and targeted cyberattack in which an intruder gains access to a network and remains undetected for an extended period.
- Phishing (see below)
- Trojan Horse is a program designed to breach the security of a computer system while ostensibly performing some innocuous function.

- Botnets is a network of private computers infected with malicious software and controlled as a group without the owners' knowledge

- Ransomware is a type of malicious software designed to block access to a computer system until a sum of money is paid.

- Distributed Denial of Service (DDoS) is the intentional paralyzing of a computer network by flooding it with data sent simultaneously from many individual computer

- Wiper Attacks is a malware with intentions to wipe the hard drive of the computer it infects.

- Intellectual Property Theft involves robbing people or companies of their ideas, inventions, and creative expression.

- Data Manipulation/Destruction

- Spyware/Malware is any software intentionally designed to cause damage to a computer, server or computer network.

- Man-in-the-Middle (MITM) is an attack where the attacker secretly relays and possibly alters the communication between two parties who believe they are directly communicating with each other.

- Drive-By Downloads is the unintentional downloading of a virus or malicious software onto your computer or mobile device, usually taking advantage of a browser, app, or operating system that is out of date and has a security flaw.

- Malvertising is the practice of incorporating malware in online advertisements.

- Rogue Software is a form of malicious software and Internet fraud that misleads users into believing there is a virus on their computer and manipulates them into paying money for a fake malware removal tool.

Phishing

Mentioned in the list of attacks we explain it separately because it is easier to accomplish. The deceitful operational practice of using email, telephone or text messages alleging to be from reputable companies to induce individuals to reveal their personal information, such as passwords and credit card numbers is defined as Phishing. The information collected from phishing is most often used to access personal or corporate accounts as first steps to identity theft or financial fraud. Ways to evaluate if your communications have phishing characteristics:

1. Too Good - lucrative offers that are attention-grabbing for emotional responses immediately by clicking the link.

   Don't click on any suspicious emails.

2. Urgency - A fast response is required due to a limited time. It's an attempt get updated personal details for accounts without other measures. When in doubt, visit the source directly rather than clicking a link in an email.

3. Hyperlinks - Hovering over a link shows you the actual URL (link address) where you will be directed. The link closely mirrors a popular website with a misspelling.

4. Attachments – These documents are included in emails from unexpected or unusual senders, requiring it to be opened. They contain payloads that release sources like ransomware or other viruses. The only file type that is always safe to click on is a .txt file.

Evaluating these characteristics will allow coverage for your digital footprint but it's not as secure as needed. The traces left behind by end-user errors and risky activity are inevitably noticed.

Brute Force

A brute force attack is a trial-and-error method used to obtain information such as a user password or personal identification number (PIN). In a brute force attack, automated software is used to generate as many consecutive guesses associated to the value of the desired data. Brute force attacks may be used to crack encrypted data. A form of brute force is the dictionary attack. The hacker tries all the words in a dictionary to unlock access to a device or server. Other forms of brute force attacks attempt commonly-used passwords or combinations of letters and numbers to crack security protocols. Brute forces attacks are time and resource consuming. The success of a brute force attack is usually correlated to computing power and amount of combinations tried.

Computer to Footprint

A computer virus is a piece of code that can copy itself and typically has a detrimental effect, such as corrupting the system or destroying data. The computer virus loaded onto a computer without the end-user's knowledge is to perform malicious actions. Because threats and virus are lurking out on the internet it's important to protect your computer and the eventual spread to your digital footprint because those traces are the gateways to accessing your personal profile.

Digital Footprints

A digital footprint, like a dossier kept on a person, is the outline of information existing from the actions and communications conducted online. A digital footprint can be traced back to a specific individual in two formats.

Active –

Active footprints are shadow traces the end-user leaves intentionally. With each engagement or communications on Facebook, Twitter and blog posts or other social networks the entries into the dossier is active.

Passive –

Passive footprints are shadow traces connected to the end-user through third-party activities. With each engagement or communication with retail or other franchises it adds passive traces

Protecting yourself requires that you take control over the things you can control and managing the responses to the things you cannot control.

Creating Footprints

In decades passed, your status could be formulated from your practical experiences and the records of accomplishments like your resume or transcripts. In our current state related to the technological age, the digital footprint is becoming everything those documents represented. For those generations where technology is not a tool but a natural element of their lives, the importance to guard it is not exaggerated. With the shift in the importance of defining (not to mention the valuing) of us through our digital footprint, is more than a trend. Data availability becoming continuous and instantaneous, projects that not having a digital footprint will equate no presence. The unique characteristic of an individual's digital footprint is becoming even more complex as it intertwines the values of other individuals' footprints. The need to create access points to digital footprints lead to the unparallel use of algorithms to analyze against other footprints. It's critical to monitor and reframe your digital footprint as necessary, it's almost becoming required to have footprint ambassadors.

Footprint Duration

There much debated information about erasing online information; however, the shadow trace of a digital footprint is permanent. In some cases; the information is hidden from public or semi-public access however, never deleted like many perceive. The shadow traces allow others to control the information and leaves the owner (of the interaction) little to no regulation over the future use or dissemination of the information.

Differentiate Footprints

With the knowledge of digital footprint being permanent; it should create a heightened expectation for making or keeping it as a constructive element. There are only points to differentiate in footprints, positive and/or negative.

Negative Footprints

A negative digital footprint consists of things that are accessible on the internet that you might regret later. These images, words or associations could be something inappropriate or misguided. For the misinformed individual's, an extraordinary amount of your digital footprint is also accessible to local law enforcement, IRS investigators, the FBI and private attorneys. The incredible part is, it can be used against you in legal matters by these agencies or the identifying information also can be intentionally sold to third parties. The least discussed use of negative footprint's is potential employers now have access to the information as well.

Positive Footprints

For a positive digital footprint, it is simply the opposite of creating the negative footprint, but we go into deeper details in the footprint management section below.

Footprint Management

To support, manage, and maintain your digital footprint there are some rudiment checks to complete:

- ✓ Search yourself online:

    Frequently view your profile through a web search by name on several platforms. If you find something you aren't happy with, take the necessary steps to get that content removed. Social media pages appear because privacy settings are not turned on.

- ✓ Check privacy settings:

    Understand what information is shared on websites you frequent. Keep in mind others that you're connected too, their content and their settings affect your digital footprint also.

✓ Think before you post:

Before you post, repost or like any information THINK, by

answering these internal questions:

T = is it true?

H = is it helpful?

I = is it inspiring?

N = is it necessary?

K = is it kind?

*** Once it is published, potentially it is there forever.

✓ Deactivate and delete:

When the use of social media profile is terminated, it's a

recommended practice to deactivate or delete the account.

Effectively moving information from active to passive and harder to access.

✓ Make a positive footprint:

The negative footprints already get plenty of attention. Keeping your digital footprint positive takes intentionally preparation and interactions while online.

Footprint Strategies

Digital footprints don't merely attract the interest of hackers or those out to steal your identity. They can also be traced by potential employers, schools, or creditors. Managing your identity clearly matters. There are a few steps that can help protect your digital footprint best as possible. The suggested steps include:

Enter your name into several search engines.

Double-check your privacy settings, but don't trust them.

Create strong, memorable passwords.

Keep all your software up to date.

Review your mobile use: if you don't need it, delete it.

Build your reputation through your behavior.

Everyone can contribute to their own positive and professional digital footprint. The actions taken when tweeting, posting or snapping contribute to the image painted about you. This painting is a snapshot of your life but can influence your employer, bank, or a college's perception of you. The best strategy is the simplest ones to accomplish; ignore negative interactions, "un-tag" your profile from questionable communications & images and keep sensitive comments off the internet. Attempt to build your digital footprint around your work, hobbies, events you're passionate about with people you can trust, and it will become second nature to behave positive digitally.

Although measures are available to thwart the government and other

agencies from monitoring your data and movements, most of your online

activity can be used, sold and shared to create a remarkably detailed

portrait of our lives. SOMETHING TO REMEMBER!

Outroduction

Knowledge Bank

The writings on the wall, learning has moved beyond the classroom walls; the opportunity to earn merit badges as you participate in the Lincoln & Hill Training digital program. To broaden your Knowledge Bank, at any moment; a multitude of experiences (**XPs**) can be collected and accomplished through the Lincoln & Hill Training platform.

Byte Marks (***Merit Badge***).

Along your learning journey you will achieve **XPs** with correlated merit badges that unlock opportunities, to stack skills. In addition, earning Lincoln & Hill Training's merit badges indicates you've completed steps across our training program. The completing of merit badges display initiative to attain 21st Century skills. Once achieved the credentials may be displayed on your social media profiles to highlight your accomplishments.

Here's how you can get started:

STEP 1 – Based on your affiliation with Lincoln & Hill Training, you will receive an invitation from us regarding your LRNG user/learner account. (*sometimes these invites get bumped to JUNK/SPAM folders, too). Register.

STEP 2 - Once you've registered,

go to https://www.lrng.org/o/lincoln-hill-training.

STEP 3 - Discover various **XPs** to complete. These are related to the different Lincoln & Hill Training suite series.

STEP 4 – Completing each **XP** unlocks new opportunities. When **XPs** are linked together they form a ***Playlist***, and once approved, you get the credentials, in the form of a ***Merit Badge***. Accomplish **XPs** and attain ***Merit Badges*** from your mobile device or laptop. Not only are you developing your skills and network, but you are also growing a portfolio of experiences. Each credential can be uploaded to your LinkedIn account to share with your professional network.

Workbook

The questions below reflect some of the most common areas related to any of the Byte Marks: traces from digital footprint sessions. Answer all questions. **Discuss & Share** your answers with your cohort to provide understanding for each of your responses. Make additional notes if questions/concern aren't answered immediately, information provided in later sessions will help you get clarification plus provide scriptural cross-referencing.

Questions

 (Digital Divide Tag)

1. In what ways is continuous access or lack of access affecting the growing phenomenon of digital footprints? Be specific

 **(Investigate Tag)**

1. Which of the principles introduced in Byte Marks do you need to investigate further to help yourself? Explain your answer

Illicit Behavior Tag

1. It is commonly believed the internet always for anonymity, are there illicit behaviors you're committing that there's a trace out there? Would you be interested in learning more information to clean up those traces? Be specific

(Watchman Tag)

1. Are there any young people (family or non-family) that closely follow or watch the ways your building your digital footprint? If so, how? Be specific

Self-Discipline Tag

1. In what ways are you protecting or destroying your digital footprint?

Explain your answer

Playing the Fool Tag

1. Many times the behaviors of others have a negative effect on you, are you playing to fool as an collaborator in the digital footprint of a friend, associate or family member? What steps can you take to remove yourself and get back to a positive digital footprint?

Under the Radar Tag

1. In certain situations, your digital footprint is seemingly off the grid; however, it's never really. Do you know how to minimize the exposure of your digital footprint? Explain your answer

Practical Exercise

 Practical Exercise Tag

In the four (4) categories list some situations or people that are creating

information that effects your digital footprint.

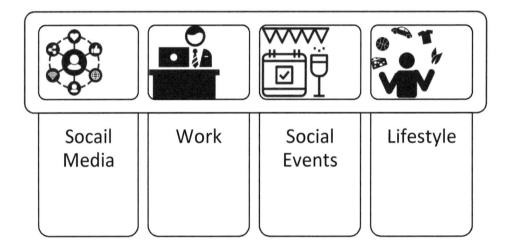

Socail Media	Work	Social Events	Lifestyle

www.ingramcontent.com/pod-product-compliance
Lightning Source LLC
Chambersburg PA
CBHW041432050326
40690CB00002B/512